Buckle Down!™
on
AMERICAN CITIZENSHIP

Third Edition

Buckle Down
PUBLISHING COMPANY

Third Edition

ISBN 0-7836-1358-X

Catalog #BD OH9C 1

7 8 9 10

Dear Student,

The Ohio State Board of Education requires every student to pass a citizenship test before graduating from high school. If you do not pass it in ninth grade, you may try again later. The Ohio Department of Education will let you take the test twice a year. You must pass this test in order to receive a high school diploma.

Did you ever study *citizenship*? Sure you did. You probably had an American history class in 5th or 6th grade. You can probably find Ohio on a map of the United States. You know something about voting and elections. Actually, most of what you need to know for your citizenship test has already been presented to you at some time or another. The problem is, people forget–teachers forget, parents forget, and even students forget. So, what's the point? Why not just forget it. Allow me to repeat myself . . .

> *If you do not pass the state citizenship test, you will not receive a high school diploma.*

It may sound strange to you, but *it is against the law* for your high school to give you a diploma if you don't pass the proficiency test. If you pass it in the ninth grade, you won't need to worry about it later.

This third edition of *Buckle Down on American Citizenship* is an improved version of the book that helped thousands of students pass the state test. It reviews important topics and concepts in each category covered by the state. The program provides review activities and a few practice questions. Even though the third edition is improved, YOU still have to do the work.

Sincerely,

Bud C. Wonkle
Editor-in-Chief

The third edition of *Buckle Down on American Citizenship* is based on the design of the Ohio Citizenship Test. The state test covers six social studies categories. Within these six categories, seventeen different learning outcomes are tested.

HIGH SCHOOL PROFICIENCY TESTING: NINTH-GRADE CITIZENSHIP LEARNING OUTCOMES

The learning outcomes of the Ohio State Board of Education are provided below.

1. Identify the major significance of the following historic documents: Northwest Ordinance, Declaration of Independence, Constitution, Bill of Rights.

2. Know that many different peoples with diverse backgrounds (cultural, racial, ethnic, linguistic), make up our nation today.

3. Identify various symbols of the United States: flag, national anthem, Pledge of Allegiance, Independence Day.

4. Locate the United States, the nation's capital, the state of Ohio, and Ohio's capital on appropriate maps of the nation, hemisphere, or world.

5. Demonstrate map-reading skills, including finding directions, judging distances, and reading the legend.

6. Know the following economic concepts:
   a. All levels of U.S. government assess taxes in order to provide services.
   b. Individuals and societies make choices to satisfy wants with limited resources.
   c. Nations become interdependent through trade.

7. Identify the main functions of each branch of government (executive, legislative, judicial) at the national, state, and local levels.

8. Identify major economic systems: capitalism, socialism, communism.

9. Demonstrate an understanding of the concept of federalism by identifying the level of government (local, state, national) responsible for addressing the concerns of citizens.

10. Distinguish the characteristics, both positive and negative, of various types of government: representative democracy, monarchy, dictatorship.

11. Describe the process for making, amending, or removing laws.

12. Know how the law protects individuals in the United States.

13. Understand that the major role of political parties in a democracy is to provide a choice in governmental leadership (i.e., candidates and platforms).

14. Understand the role of public officials in government.

15. Know that voting is both a privilege and a responsibility of U.S. citizenship.

16. Demonstrate the ability to use information that enables citizens to make informed choices.

17. Identify opportunities for involvement in civic activities.

HISTORY

UNIT 1

citizenship review

Within the category of history, the Ohio State Department of Education expects you to know about the following topics:

1. Historic Documents

Identify the significance of the following historic documents:

- Northwest Ordinance
- Declaration of Independence
- U.S. Constitution
- Bill of Rights

2. American Diversity

Know that many different peoples with diverse backgrounds make up our nation today. Areas of study include:

- early immigrants to the U.S.
- contributions of racial and ethnic groups
- influences on language and culture

3. Symbols of the United States

Identify various symbols of the United States:

- American flag
- National Anthem
- Pledge of Allegiance
- Independence Day

1. Historic Documents

The following four documents have more than historical importance. They provide the foundation for government and law in our country and protect the rights of individuals. The purpose and content of each document is summarized below.

The Declaration of Independence – 1776

This document declared the independence of the American colonies from Great Britain. **Thomas Jefferson**, who wrote most of the Declaration, developed the following argument for independence.

- People have basic rights, including life, liberty, and the pursuit of happiness.

- The function of government is to protect and serve these rights. If the government fails to do this, the people have a right to seek change.

- Great Britain, under King George, was not serving the colonists' rights; therefore, the colonists had a right to declare their independence.

The Declaration of Independence continues to serve today as the basic statement of our nation's political philosophy.

The Northwest Ordinance – 1787

This document provided **guidelines** for settling and governing the **Northwest Territory**, an area lying north of the Ohio and Mississippi Rivers (see map). The **Ordinance** served as a model for governing other territories. Main features of the Ordinance included:

- A process for requesting **statehood**. Ohio became the first state, followed by Wisconsin, Michigan, Illinois, and Indiana.

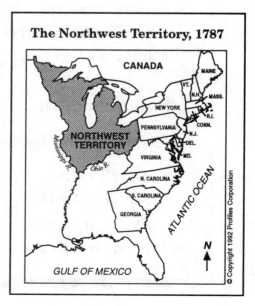

The Northwest Territory, 1787

- A guarantee of trial by jury, public education, and freedom of religion for residents of the territory.

- The **prohibition** of slavery in the territory and newly formed states.

The United States Constitution – 1787

The **Constitution**, with its **amendments**, is a set of laws that serves as the written plan for our government. It defines which powers are held by the **federal** government and which by the states. It limits the power of government by giving certain powers to each of the three **branches**.

- The **legislative branch** has the power to make laws.

- The **executive branch** has the power to enforce laws.

- The **judicial branch** has the power to interpret laws.

This is called **separation of powers**. Each branch limits the power of the other branches through a system of **checks and balances**.

The Bill of Rights – 1791

The Bill of Rights is composed of the first ten amendments to the Constitution. It was written to protect the rights of ordinary Americans by identifying individual rights that cannot be taken away. Some of these rights include:

- freedom of speech

- freedom of religion

- freedom of **assembly**

- trial by jury

- the right to a lawyer

The Bill of Rights also states that all powers of government not **delegated** to the federal government are **reserved** for the states. The sharing of power between the federal and state governments is called **federalism**.

Every American should be familiar with the **Preamble** to the Constitution:

We, the people of the United States, in order to form a more perfect Union, establish justice, insure domestic tranquility, provide for the common defense, promote the general welfare, and secure the blessings of liberty to ourselves and our posterity, do ordain and establish this Constitution for the United States of America.

FOR CLASS DISCUSSION

1. What do the Declaration of Independence, the Northwest Ordinance, the Constitution, and the Bill of Rights have in common?

2. How do these documents differ?

3. How do these documents affect the lives of Americans today?

4. Which freedoms guaranteed by the Bill of Rights have become issues in the news in recent years?

2. American Diversity

The United States often has been called a **"nation of nations."** The people of our country come from many different racial, cultural, and ethnic backgrounds. A short list includes the various cultures of the Native Americans who have lived here for thousands of years; the colonial cultures of England, Spain, France, Germany, and the Netherlands; and the African cultures originally brought by slaves. Later immigrants from China, Ireland, Italy, and Eastern Europe added to our nation's cultural variety. In the latter part of the 20th century, migrations from Asia and Latin America have greatly influenced our way of life.

English became the main language and dominant culture of our country because the majority of early settlers came from Great Britain and Ireland. Our laws are also based largely on English law.

All of these cultures have added something to the mix of language, customs, food, clothing, art, and other traditions we call American culture. That is why the United States is often referred to as the **melting pot**.

Immigrants influenced the progress of our country in other ways, too. They formed the **labor pool** for the Industrial Revolution and helped build canals and railroads for **westward expansion**.

People still come to the United States for many of the same reasons they always have: job opportunities, a higher standard of living, freedom of expression and religions, and a democratic government.

Activity: Origins of everyday words

Our vocabulary is filled with words from other languages. Below are words contributed by African Americans (AA), Native Americans (NA), Spanish (S), and German (G) immigrants. For each word, indicate its origin by writing the abbreviation beside each word.

barbecue	jazz	burrito	frankfurter
pretzel	safari	ranch	canoe
Ohio	rodeo	Monongahela	Illinois

FOR CLASS DISCUSSION

Some people say the United States is not so much a "melting pot" as a "salad bowl."

1. How do these two nicknames differ in meaning?

2. Give an example of something that supports the "melting pot" version of our nation's diversity.

3. Give an example of something that supports the "salad bowl" version of the U.S.

3. Symbols of the United States

The Flag of the United States

George Washington raised the first U.S. flag on January 1, 1776. Congress approved the form of the present U.S. flag on June 14, 1777. A decision was made in 1818 that the 13 red and white stripes, representing the original 13 colonies, would always remain the same. A white star would be added to represent each state. Our flag currently has 50 stars, representing the 50 U.S. States.

The National Anthem

Our national **anthem**, the **Star Spangled Banner**, was written by **Francis Scott Key**. Key composed the song during the War of 1812 between the U.S. and Great Britain. Key was being held on a British warship during the shelling of Fort McHenry in 1814. Legend has it that when the bombing stopped, Key was so moved to see the American flag still flying that he wrote the first verse, beginning with, "Oh, say can you see." The song didn't officially become our national anthem until 1916, by order of **President Woodrow Wilson**. Congress approved the decision in 1931.

The Pledge of Allegiance

U.S. citizens express their loyalty to our country and its democratic ideals by reciting the Pledge of Allegiance to the flag. **Francis Bellamy** wrote the pledge, which follows, in 1892.

I pledge allegiance to the flag of the United States of America, and to the Republic, for which it stands, one nation, under God, indivisible, with liberty and justice for all.

The Fourth of July

The Fourth of July, or Independence Day, has been celebrated as a holiday in this country since the American Revolution. The holiday commemorates, or honors, the signing of the Declaration of Independence on July 4, 1776.

FOR CLASS DISCUSSION

---

1. A **symbol** is an object, image, or event that stands for something else, such as a quality, emotion, or ideal. Explain, in a word or phrase, what each of the following symbols represents.

   - The U.S. Flag

   - The Fourth of July

   - The Pledge of Allegiance

   - The National Anthem

2. What other types of symbols might represent America, or the American way of life, to people in other parts of the world?

3. From time to time, a singer will generate controversy with his or her version of the Star Spangled Banner. The two sides of the argument usually take the form of "freedom of expression" vs. "respect for a national symbol." Is one side right? Or do both sides have something positive to say about our country?

Questions for Review

A. Vocabulary

_____ 1. protects freedom of individual

_____ 2. a system to limit powers of government branches

_____ 3. a statement of loyalty

_____ 4. led to statehood for Ohio

_____ 5. a mix of cultures

_____ 6. a person from one country who settles in another

_____ 7. opening paragraph of the Constitution

_____ 8. Star Spangled Banner

_____ 9. supreme law of the U.S.

_____ 10. July 4, 1776

A. national anthem

B. melting pot

C. immigrant

D. Independence Day

E. Bill of Rights

F. checks and balances

G. Constitution

H. Pledge of Allegiance

I. Preamble

J. Northwest Ordinance

B. Completion

1. The main author of the Declaration of Independence was _____.

2. The three branches of government are the _____, the _____, and the _____.

3. The number of stripes on the American flag is _____. The number of stars is _____.

4. The Bill of Rights is composed of the _____ to the Constitution.

5. The Declaration of Independence is based on the idea that all people have a right to _____, _____, and _____.

6. The Northwest Ordinance prohibited _____ in any part of the Northwest Territory.

C. Short Answer

1. Name three rights that are protected by the Bill of Rights.

   _____

2. What is the purpose of a system of checks and balances in a government?

   _____

3. What do the stars and stripes on the American flag represent?

   _____

4. Why is American culture known as a "melting pot"?

   _____

5. Why did English become the main language of our country?

   _____

D. True or False

_____ 1. The Declaration of Independence is part of the Constitution.

_____ 2. Americans have celebrated the Fourth of July for over 200 years.

_____ 3. Francis Scott Key wrote the Pledge of Allegiance.

_____ 4. The Bill of Rights was written to protect the power of the government.

_____ 5. A star is added to the flag whenever a new state joins the nation.

E. Multiple Choice

1. The executive branch of government is primarily responsible for
    A. writing and passing new laws.
    B. conducting fair trials.
    C. enforcing laws.
    D. interpreting the Constitution.

2. Which of the following states was not part of the Northwest Territory?
    A. North Dakota
    B. Illinois
    C. Michigan
    D. Wisconsin

3. Which of the following is NOT true of the Declaration of Independence?
    A. It rejected the rule of Great Britain and King George.
    B. It defined the laws that would serve as a plan for our government.
    C. It formally declared the colonies as independent states.
    D. It stated that government should serve individual rights.

Extended Activities

1. Historic Documents

Read more information on the events surrounding the writing and signing of the Declaration of Independence. Then write a scene as if it were part of a play about the Declaration of Independence. Before you write, think about the following questions: Who is the cast of characters in the scene you have chosen? What are these people like? What is happening in this scene? What is the general mood of the scene?

2. American Diversity

A. Read more information on Ellis Island in New York harbor, where most immigrants entered the United States from 1892 to 1943. Choose a year between 1892 and 1943. Find out what nationalities of immigrants were most likely to have entered the United States that year. Imagine that you are an employee of the government working on Ellis Island during the year you have chosen. You are processing a boatload of immigrants. What country are they from? What is the immigration process like? To what new homes will these people most likely go from here?

B. Research the history of your town/city/county. What Native American tribes have lived there? When was it settled by immigrants? Who were the first settlers? Were any battles fought over the territory? What ethnic or cultural groups are represented there today? What types of agriculture, industry, or commerce are most common? Use this information to write a brief account of the history of your area to pass on to your descendants. Be sure to describe your family's role in the history of the community, whether long-term or very recent.

3. Symbols of the United States

Imagine that you are the head of a committee creating a time capsule to be filled with symbols of the United States and the American way of life. What should go in the time capsule?

Test Writers' Workshop

Read the passage below, then complete questions 1–3.

In 1787, under the Articles of Confederation, the young American government set forth a plan for creating future states. By act of Congress, the Northwest Ordinance divided a large area of land called the Northwest Territory into smaller territorial units. These separate territories would later become equal partners with New York, Virginia, Pennsylvania, and the other original members of the Union.

The Northwest Territory was bordered by the Ohio River to the east, the Mississippi River to the west, and the Great Lakes to the north.

According to the Ordinance, until an area achieved statehood, a governor, three judges, and a secretary would be appointed to preside over its affairs. The Ordinance also specified that the population in a territory would determine its eligibility to join the Union. A territory could not elect a legislature until 5000 eligible voters had settled there. Statehood could only become a reality when a territory reached a population of 60,000 eligible voters. (At that time in America's history, the term "eligible voters" referred only to adult white males.) Once a territory achieved statehood, it was then guaranteed equal status with all other states in the Union.

Today's states of Ohio, Indiana, Illinois, Michigan, and Wisconsin got their beginnings under the Northwest Ordinance. The northeastern portion of the state of Minnesota was also included in the Northwest Territory.

Complete the following multiple-choice test question about the reading passage by creating the missing answer choices.

1. The land in which of the following states was entirely a part of the Northwest Territory?

   A. _____

   B. _____

   C. _____

   D. _____

   Hint: Start with a correct answer: for example, Ohio. Then, write three false answers using the names of other states mentioned in the passage that were not entirely a part of the Northwest Territory.

Write another test question that gives one of the following responses as the correct answer.

2. _____

   _____

   A. form its own legislature
   B. leave the Northwest Territory
   C. gain full statehood
   D. define its borders

Now write a complete multiple-choice item using the information in the reading passage.

3. _____

   _____

   A. _____

   B. _____

   C. _____

   D. _____

14

GEOGRAPHY

citizenship review

Within the category of geography, the Ohio State Department of Education expects you to know about the following topics:

1. Place Locations on Maps

Given an appropriate map of the world, hemisphere, or nation, students will need to be able to locate:

- the United States
- the nation's capital, Washington, D.C.
- the state of Ohio
- Ohio's capital, Columbus

2. Map-reading Skills

Students will be required to demonstrate map-reading skills, including:

- finding directions
- judging distances between points using a scale
- reading a legend

1. Place Locations on Maps

Finding places on maps is easier if you remember that some maps give the big picture, while others give closer views of a particular area.

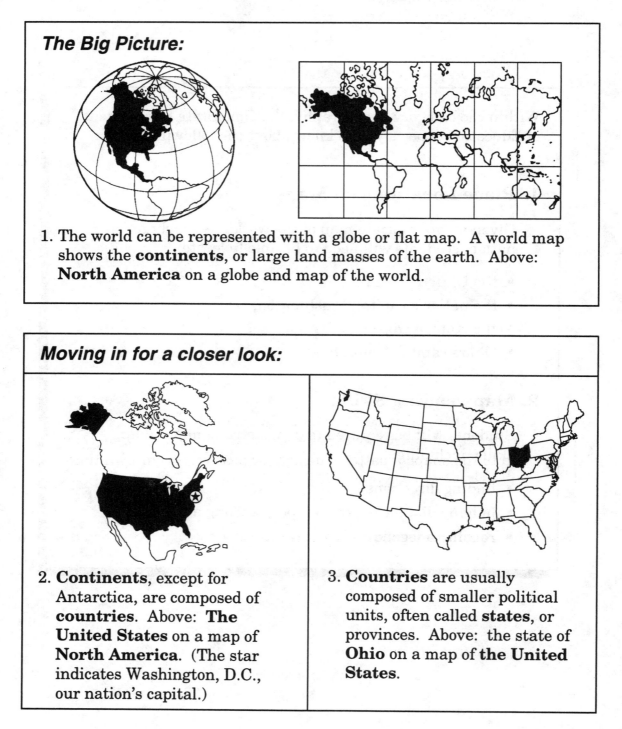

The Big Picture:

1. The world can be represented with a globe or flat map. A world map shows the **continents**, or large land masses of the earth. Above: **North America** on a globe and map of the world.

Moving in for a closer look:

2. **Continents**, except for Antarctica, are composed of **countries**. Above: **The United States** on a map of **North America**. (The star indicates Washington, D.C., our nation's capital.)

3. **Countries** are usually composed of smaller political units, often called **states**, or provinces. Above: the state of **Ohio** on a map of **the United States**.

Close-up

4. **States** in our country are usually composed of **counties**, which contain **towns or villages** and **cities**. Right: **Columbus**, the capital of the state, and some other major cities in Ohio.

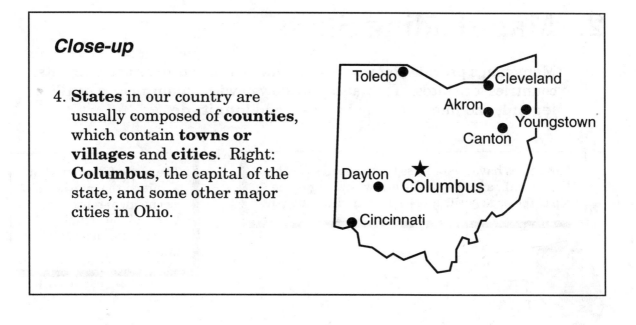

Activities:

1. If you were mailing a letter to another planet, how would you write your return address?

2. Remembering places is largely a matter of remembering shapes. Trace the shapes of North America, the U.S., and/or Ohio, then add to the shape a pattern, design, or picture of your own that will help you to remember it in the future.

2. Map-reading Skills

Many maps provide you with more than just the outlines of continents, countries, or states. They also provide you with a **compass**, a **scale**, a **legend**, and lines marking **latitude** and **longitude**.

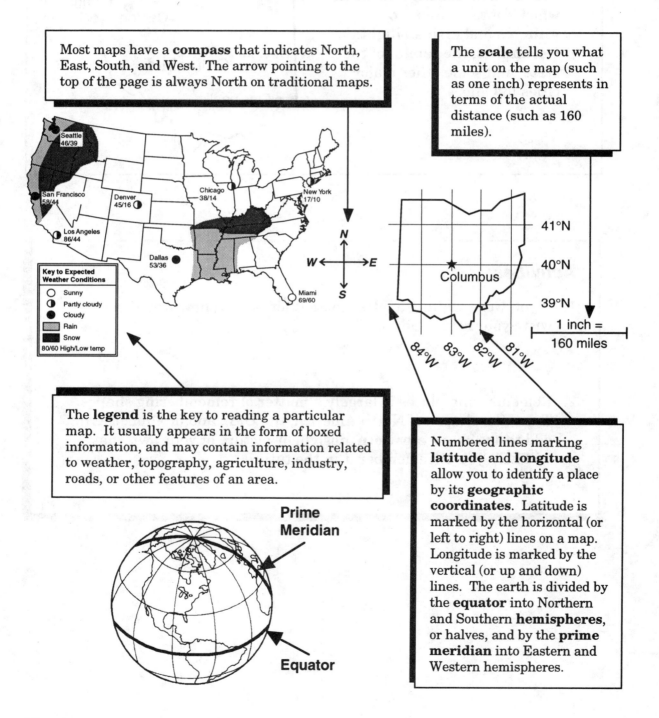

Most maps have a **compass** that indicates North, East, South, and West. The arrow pointing to the top of the page is always North on traditional maps.

The **scale** tells you what a unit on the map (such as one inch) represents in terms of the actual distance (such as 160 miles).

The **legend** is the key to reading a particular map. It usually appears in the form of boxed information, and may contain information related to weather, topography, agriculture, industry, roads, or other features of an area.

Numbered lines marking **latitude** and **longitude** allow you to identify a place by its **geographic coordinates**. Latitude is marked by the horizontal (or left to right) lines on a map. Longitude is marked by the vertical (or up and down) lines. The earth is divided by the **equator** into Northern and Southern **hemispheres**, or halves, and by the **prime meridian** into Eastern and Western hemispheres.

Prime Meridian

Equator

Activities:

1. Draw a simplified map of your school and school grounds. Include a compass, a scale (estimated measurements will do), and a simple legend that describes some feature (such as different areas of activity) of your school.

2. Locate your hometown on the map on the preceding page, then determine what its geographic coordinates (latitude and longitude) would be.

Questions for Review

A. Vocabulary

_____ 1. one of the large land masses of the earth

_____ 2. one-half of the earth

_____ 3. indicates direction on a map

_____ 4. the key, usually boxed, to reading information on a particular map

_____ 5. identification of place by latitudinal and longitudinal markings

_____ 6. divides the earth into northern and southern hemispheres

_____ 7. a city or town that serves as the seat of government for a state or nation

_____ 8. one of the 50 territorial and political units that make up the U.S.

_____ 9. divides the earth into eastern and western hemispheres

_____ 10. tells you what a unit on a map represents in terms of actual distance

A. scale

B. capital

C. equator

D. state

E. continent

F. hemisphere

G. compass

H. prime meridian

I. geographic coordinates

J. legend

B. Completion

1. The capital of Ohio is _____.

2. Our nation's capital is _____.

3. The United States is part of the continent of _____.

4. The horizontal lines marking locations north and south on the globe are called

    lines of _____ . The vertical lines marking east and west locations

    are called lines of _____ .

C. True or False

_____ 1. Washington, D.C., is located on the west coast of the United States.

_____ 2. Cleveland is the capital of Ohio.

_____ 3. On traditional maps, the arrow at the top of the compass points North.

_____ 4. The legend on a map is used to represent distances.

_____ 5. Ohio touches the northern border of the United States.

D. Ordering – Use your geographic knowledge to arrange the following in order, from smallest to largest, beginning with line 1.

A. hemisphere

B. country

C. city

D. continent

E. state

5. _____

4. _____

3. _____

2. _____

1. _____

E. Map reading – Study the following map, then answer the questions that follow.

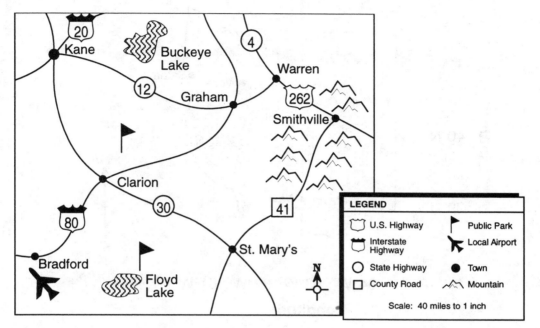

1. Which lake is located next to a public park?

   _____

2. Which state highway generally runs east and west?

   _____

3. Graham and Clarion are about two inches apart on this map. How far apart are they in terms of actual miles?

   _____

4. If you lived in Kane, and someone asked directions to the airport, what would you tell him/her? Be specific.

   _____

5. Which two towns are connected by a county road?

   _____

6. If you wanted to drive from St. Mary's to Graham without driving through the mountains, which roads would you take? Be specific.

   _____

Use the map below to answer questions 7–12.

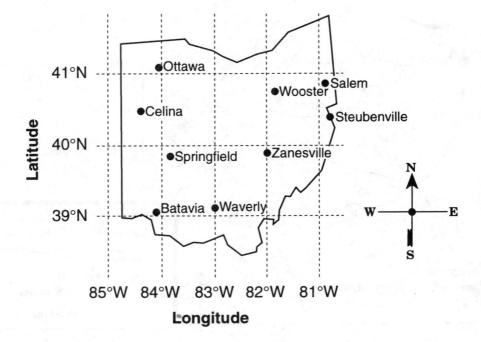

7. Which city or cities are southwest of Zanesville?

_____

8. Which city is northwest of Wooster?

_____

9. Which city is farthest east?

_____

10. Which city is closest to 40°N 84°W?

_____

11. What latitude and longitude is Salem closest to?

_____

12. Describe Celina's location in terms of latitude and longitude.

_____

Use the map below to answer questions 13–18.

13. What physical feature lies between the two major mountain ranges in the western part of the United States?

_____

14. Name three physical features found along the southern border of the United States.

_____

15. What physical feature is found just north of both of the swamp regions?

_____

16. In what *general* directions do the major mountain ranges run?

_____

17. What is the predominating physical feature in the United States?

_____

18. What physical feature is found in most of Ohio?

_____

Extended Activities

1. Place Locations on Maps

A. Draw a map that places your town or city in the county where it resides. Use an appropriate scale, indicate major highways around your town, show physical features, locate nearby towns, create a legend, and draw a directional compass for your map.

B. If available, play the computer game "Where in the World is Carmen San Diego?" with your class. (This Macintosh-compatible geography game is available in many school libraries. To play the game, you'll need to look up information in reference books in order to solve a mystery.) One computer can run the program in front of the class, but your teacher may need to read the information on the screen aloud. Divide the class into small groups to work as detective teams.

Each team should attempt to solve the mystery by following the clues given. At various places in the game, the teams will have to come to an agreement about what to do next. A simple majority vote of the teams can determine the next step. The first team to solve the mystery is declared the winner. Each group will need access to an almanac and world map or atlas. Other reference sources, such as an encyclopedia and a dictionary, may also be helpful.

2. Map-Reading Skills

Create a secret message to trade with another student. Use latitude and longitude clues to create a secret message using the first letters of the names of countries on the globe. For example, 20°S 140°E is located in Australia, so the clue is 20°S 140°E and the answer is the letter "A."

Test Writers' Workshop

Use the map of the western hemisphere for questions 1–3.

Complete the following multiple-choice test question about the map of the western hemisphere by creating the missing answer choices.

1. If you were to take a direct flight from Mexico City to Brasilia, which direction would you travel?

    A. _____

    B. _____

    C. _____

    D. _____

    Hint: Use the compass to determine the correct answer choice, then write three false choices.

Now write two more complete multiple-choice items using the information in the map.

2. _____

    _____

    A. _____

    B. _____

    C. _____

    D. _____

3. _____

    _____

    A. _____

    B. _____

    C. _____

    D. _____

ECONOMICS

UNIT 3

citizenship review

Within the category of economics, the Ohio State Department of Education expects you to know about the following topics.

1. Economic Concepts

Know the following concepts:

- **Taxes:** All levels of U.S. government assess taxes in order to provide services.
- **Scarcity:** Individuals and societies must make choices to satisfy wants with limited resources.
- **Trade:** Nations become interdependent through trade.

2. Major Economic Systems

Know the definitions, characteristics, and differences among three major economic systems and the differences among those systems.

- Capitalism
- Socialism
- Communism

1. Economic Concepts

You need an understanding of the following three basic economic issues.

Taxes

Everyone in the United States, including students and people who are not citizens, must pay some **taxes**. Taxes pay for the services provided by our **federal**, **state**, and **local** governments. Those services include national defense, public education, economic development, parks, courts, and police and fire protection.

Many different *kinds* of taxes are collected. Not all state and local governments collect the same taxes. Some of the most common taxes are listed in the following chart.

FEDERAL	STATE OF OHIO	LOCAL
• **income** tax (due every April) • **social security** tax • **estate** tax (paid on a deceased person's possessions if the value is over $600,000) • **customs** (tax or duty paid on goods brought into or exported from the country)	• **income** tax • **inheritance** tax • **business** tax (paid on stock transfers) • **sales** tax (paid on the purchase of some goods and services) • **license** fees	• **property** tax • **sales** tax • **license** fees (such as for dogs or fishing) • **fees** for services (such as parking) • some local governments also collect **income** tax

Scarcity

When it comes to economic problems, individuals and governments are alike in one way. They cannot always have everything they want, or even need, because they do not always have enough resources. This imbalance between our **unlimited** wants and our **limited** resources is called **scarcity**.

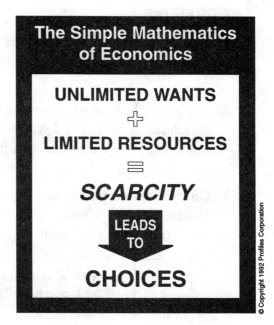

The Simple Mathematics of Economics

UNLIMITED WANTS
+
LIMITED RESOURCES
=
SCARCITY
LEADS TO
CHOICES

© Copyright 1992 Profiles Corporation

You may be most familiar with "scarcity" in terms of a lack of money. To a nation, scarcity could mean the lack of other resources, too, such as wood, coal, minerals, or skilled workers.

Scarcity forces the United States government, as well as people like you, to make choices. The government has to decide what to buy and what to produce. Every choice costs time, money, goods, and/or services. This is called the **opportunity cost**. To spend or lose one benefit in order to gain another is called a **trade-off**.

Trade

If you have a job, you trade your time, skill, and effort for money. In short, you trade something you have for something you want or need. Countries depend on trade in much the same way. Resources (such as wheat, oil, timber, or iron) are not distributed equally among countries. Countries trade or sell what they have for what they need. This results in **interdependence** among nations. The key to this type of trade is **specialization**. Most countries specialize in selling goods they can produce quickly, easily, or in quantity. The U.S., for example, produces more wheat than it can use. It sells wheat for other things it needs, such as oil.

Activities:

1. How would your community change if all tax support ended? What sites and services would disappear? What problems might occur?

2. Imagine that you have received $20 for your birthday. Apply the concepts of unlimited wants, limited resources, opportunity costs, and trade-off to the choices you might consider in spending the money.

3. Complete the following chart listing the most common kinds of taxes, the level of government that collects the tax, and the service or item on which the tax is paid.

Tax	Level of Government (Local, State, or Federal)	Service or Item Taxed
estate tax		
		fishing
sales tax		
		parking
		money a relative left you in her will
		money you earn
customs		

4. Explain the following concepts to another student. Give examples from your own life.

wants/needs	**resources**	**trade**
interdependent	**opportunity cost**	**scarcity**
choices	**trade-off**	**specialization**

5. Cut articles from newspapers that refer directly to taxes or that discuss programs which are supported by tax dollars. Identify the program or service, the kind of tax which supports the program, and the level of government at which the tax is collected.

2. Economic Systems

An economic system is the way in which a country manages the production and distribution of its goods and services. The three major economic systems are **capitalism**, **socialism**, and **communism**. The basic difference in the three systems is the ownership of property and resources.

CAPITALISM	SOCIALISM	COMMUNISM
Capitalism is an economic system based on the private ownership of property. In a capitalist society, individuals and businesses invest money in various means of production—such as factories, machines, or land—in order to gain a profit. Individuals also invest in or own the means of distribution for finished products and goods. They decide how much they will charge for those goods, although prices are largely determined by the demands of the marketplace. The United States, Canada, and many other countries have capitalist economies.	Socialism is an economic system in which the principal means of production are controlled or owned by the central government. For example, the government owns and operates major forms of industry, such as steel mills, and major resources, such as forests. In socialist economies, the government might also control major service industries, such as transportation. Individuals may own and operate small businesses. A goal of socialism is to provide all citizens with basic economic needs. Socialist ideals have influenced the economies of Great Britain, Denmark, Sweden, and many other nations.	Communism is often defined as the final stage of socialism. The goal of a communist economic system is to eliminate social classes, replace competition with cooperation, and ultimately meet the economic needs of everyone in the society. The means of economic production and distribution are owned and controlled by society as a whole (usually represented by a central government). Communism is being replaced by capitalism in many countries. For example, the former U.S.S.R., before it was disbanded, was a communist nation. The largest communist nation in the world today is China.

FOR CLASS DISCUSSION

1. What are some ways in which an individual might benefit from capitalism? from communism? from socialism?

2. What are the disadvantages to an individual of the three economic systems?

3. What role does the government play in determining a nation's economic system?

4. Complete the following chart to see the similarities and differences among the three economic systems.

	Capitalism	Socialism	Communism
1. Ownership of means of production			
2. Decisions regarding distribution of goods			
3. Ownership of land			
4. Ownership of industries			
5. Ownership of small businesses			

Questions for Review

A. Vocabulary

_____ 1. timber, water, coal, minerals

_____ 2. tax paid on money earned

_____ 3. occurs when needs cannot be met with existing resources

_____ 4. the factories and machines used to make goods

_____ 5. results when two countries rely on each other to provide needed goods

_____ 6. to lose one benefit in order to gain another

_____ 7. paid on the purchase of goods or services

_____ 8. tax paid on goods brought into or out of the country

_____ 9. a decision about balancing wants and needs

_____ 10. the total expense of time, money, and goods involved in making an economic choice

_____ 11. to exchange something you have for something you need

A. trade-off

B. trade

C. resources

D. income tax

E. opportunity cost

F. scarcity

G. choice

H. interdependence

I. sales tax

J. customs

K. means of production

B. Completion

1. The Federal government and the state of Ohio both collect _____ taxes.

2. The manner in which a country produces and distributes goods is described as its

   _____.

3. In a _____ economy, the central government makes the

   major economic decisions.

4. In a _____ economy, the law of supply and demand determines what

   goods will be produced and at what price.

5. The final stage of socialism, in which all means of production and distribution are

   controlled by the government, is _____.

C. Short Answer

1. When the government owns nearly all the means of production, what types of things does it own?

   _____

2. What type of economy does a country have when the government owns the major means of production, but not small businesses?

   _____

3. What is the main purpose for collecting taxes?

   _____

4. Explain why relatively few people pay estate taxes.

   _____

5. Why do taxpayers mark April 15 on their calendars?

_____

6. What are three examples of products that lead to economic interdependence among nations?

_____

_____

D. True or False

_____ 1. Customs, a tax on imported goods, is collected by state governments.

_____ 2. License fees for dogs and fishing are collected by the Federal government.

_____ 3. Economic scarcity is the main reason for trade among nations.

_____ 4. The socialist economic system thrives on competition among businesses.

_____ 5. States collect inheritance taxes.

_____ 6. People who live in the United States but are not citizens do not have to pay taxes.

E. Multiple Choice

1. Taxes are a primary source of support for all of the following areas **except**
   A. parks.
   B. television.
   C. education.
   D. defense.

2. Communism is based on
   A. private ownership of property and resources.
   B. government control of property and resources.
   C. competition among businesses and industries.
   D. a complex social class system.

3. Which of the following is a basic difference in the three economic systems?
   A. use of natural resources
   B. the annual production of goods
   C. dependence on foreign trade
   D. ownership of property and resources

4. Why do collectors place a higher value on some baseball cards than on others?
   A. Baseball card collectors have no other valuable objects.
   B. The means of production is controlled by the baseball commissioner.
   C. The scarcity of some baseball cards has made them valuable.
   D. The trade-off is poor.

5. What is the primary reason the United States trades with other countries?
   A. to obtain goods we do not have in our own country
   B. Most other countries' goods are superior to our own.
   C. to increase goodwill with other countries
   D. Most other countries are more industrialized.

Extended Activities

1. Economic Concepts

Draw a detailed diagram tracing the route of a grain of wheat as it is grown, travels across the world, and finally becomes a consumer product in another country. Your diagram should show:

- where it comes from (farmland somewhere in the United States),

- how it gets to the east or west coast,

- how it travels to another country (choose a country that you know buys wheat from the United States)

- where it goes once it arrives in that country (a mill? a food processing plant?) and what consumer product it becomes,

- where the customer buys the product,

- how the customer gets the product home.

Now define "interdependence" from the grain of wheat's point of view.

2. Economic Systems

A. Choose four students from your class. Have them play the part of a capitalist, a socialist, and a communist who hold a discussion with a news reporter, played by the fourth student. The reporter moderates the discussion as each person talks about the merits and drawbacks of his or her economic system.

B. Most Americans want to balance the federal budget, but few agree on how it should be done. Pretend that you are a Senator or Representative from your state. Choose one program that has been cut from the federal budget and present a case to your constituents either supporting or criticizing this cut. Use newspaper and magazine articles to support your position.

Test Writers' Workshop

Use the reading passage to develop questions 1–3.

Jerome just got a summer job as an assembly line worker in a factory that builds electric motors for vending machines. He earns $6.00 for each hour that he works. At the end of his first 40-hour work week he collects a paycheck for $195.70. This is less than the $240 he had expected to collect. When he asks the business manager why, he is told that the government expects the company to withhold some of Jerome's pay for taxes. The business manager has also kept, or withheld, some of Jerome's pay for medical insurance and union dues.

After saving most of his paycheck for his future college expenses, Jerome had hoped to have enough money left over to buy a new skateboard. Now he doesn't even have enough to buy one wheel. He decides that he will have to ask to work overtime in order to get the money he needs. The next weekend, instead of going to the lake, Jerome spends the day sorting motor parts in the company's warehouse.

Complete the following multiple-choice test question about the reading passage by creating the missing answer choices.

1. Which of the following is a **trade-off** for Jerome?

    A. _____

    B. _____

    C. _____

    D. _____

    Hint: Look in Unit 3 to find the definition of **trade-off**. That will tell you what the correct answer should be. Then look in the passage to find other attractive answers.

Now write two more complete multiple-choice items using the information in the passage.

2. _____

_____

A. _____

B. _____

C. _____

D. _____

3. _____

_____

A. _____

B. _____

C. _____

D. _____

GOVERNMENT

UNIT 4

citizenship review

Within the category of government, the Ohio State Department of Education expects you to know about the following topics:

1. Branches of Government

Identify the main branches of government (the executive, legislative, and judicial) at the national, state, and local levels. Students will be expected to understand the functions of each branch.

- The legislative branch makes laws.
- The executive branch sees that laws are carried out.
- The judicial branch interprets laws.

2. Federalism

The student will be required to demonstrate an understanding of the concept of federalism by identifying the level of government (local, state, national) responsible for addressing the concerns of citizens. The student will also be required to demonstrate an understanding of the separation of powers, including those listed below.

- powers exclusive to the national government
- powers exclusive to the state government
- powers held by both state and national governments
- powers denied to both state and national governments
- powers held by local governments in Ohio

3. Types of Government

The student will be required to distinguish the characteristics, both positive and negative, of various types of government.

- representative democracy
- monarchy
- dictatorship

4. Political Parties

The student will be expected to understand that the major role of political parties in a democracy is to provide a choice in governmental leadership. The student will need to know about the two important functions of a political party at the national level:

- to provide governmental leadership in the form of candidates;
- to provide governmental leadership in the form of platforms.

5. Role of Public Officials

The student will be required to understand the role of public officials in government. The student must be able to:

- distinguish between elected and appointed officials;
- describe the ways officials can be elected or appointed;
- evaluate the actions of public officials on the basis of a given set of criteria;
- know how public officials at national, state, and local levels acquire their offices.

1. Branches of Government

The U.S. Constitution defined the structure of our government. The Constitution divided power into three **branches**: the **legislative**, the **executive**, and the **judicial**. Each branch has a special function:

- The legislative branch makes laws.

- The executive branch enforces laws.

- The judicial branch interprets laws.

This structure, called **separation of powers**, guarantees that no one branch ever gets too powerful.

These three branches operate at each **level** of government. In addition to our **national** or **federal** government in Washington, D.C., the United States has 50 **state** governments and hundreds of **local** governments at the city and county level.

The chart below outlines how the legislative, executive, and judicial branches are represented at each level of government.

		LEVELS OF GOVERNMENT		
		Local	**State**	**National**
BRANCHES OF GOVERNMENT	**Legislative**	City or Village Council	Ohio General Assembly	U.S. Congress (Senate and House of Representatives)
	Executive	Mayor	Governor	President
	Judicial	Municipal Courts	Ohio Supreme Court and Lower Courts	Supreme Court

Activities:

1. For each of the actions listed below, decide which **branch** and **level** of government is at work. Mark an E for executive, an L for legislative, and a J for judicial. In the third column indicate the level of government: local, state, or national.

Action	Branch	Level
1. The U.S. Congress passes an anti-pollution law.		
2. The Supreme Court declares a law unconstitutional.		
3. The City Council raises the fine for littering.		
4. A Columbus police officer gives a speeding ticket.		
5. The General Assembly passes a law requiring students to pass a citizenship test.		
6. A judge finds a defendant guilty of jaywalking.		
7. The governor appoints a new public safety director.		

2. Using the government listings in the telephone directory, give an example of each of the three branches of government that work in your community at each level of government. The chart below will help you to organize your examples.

Branch	Local	State	National
Legislative			
Executive			
Judicial			

FOR CLASS DISCUSSION

1. What types of problems might occur if the chief executive at any level of government (president, governor, or mayor) had complete power over the legislative and judicial branches at that level?

2. What is the difference between "separation of powers" and "levels of government"?

2. Federalism

After the Revolutionary War, the people in the United States had to design a new government. Some people feared that too much power would be given to the national government and not enough to the individual states. Other people feared that the national government would not get enough power to do its job.

The problem was solved by dividing powers between the state and national governments. This type of political system is called **federalism**. Our Constitution uses the following terms to define the type of political power held by each level.

1. Some powers are **reserved** by the states.
2. Some powers are **delegated** by the states to the national government.
3. Some powers are **concurrent**, meaning they are shared by both the state and national governments.
4. Some powers are **denied** either the national government, the state government, or both.

The following chart describes in more detail how powers are delegated by the people, through their state governments, to the national government.

★ ★

Our Government's Source of Power: THE PEOPLE

"We the People of the United States . . .	*do ordain and establish this Constitution*	*for the United States of America."*
We delegate power ➡	through the Constitution ➡	to the Federal Government.

© Copyright 1992 Profiles Corporation

Activities

1. Decide which levels of government would be responsible for the
   following situations. Write an F for federal, an S for state, or an
   L for local on the line provided. In some cases, two levels of
   government could be involved.

   _____ 1. Minting a new type of silver dollar.

   _____ 2. Deciding to pave a gravel road with asphalt.

   _____ 3. Opening a new post office.

   _____ 4. Issuing a marriage license.

   _____ 5. Taking military action against another country.

   _____ 6. Chartering a new bank.

   _____ 7. Registering eligible voters.

FOR CLASS DISCUSSION

1. Why are federal powers known as "delegated" powers?

2. Why are powers held by the states known as "reserved" powers?

3. What is the difference between "separation of powers" and
   "federalism"?

3. Types of Government

Every nation has a government, but not all governments are the same. Three of the most common types of government are described here:

Representative Democracy

A **democracy** is a government run by the people, either directly or indirectly. In a **representative democracy**, such as the U.S., people elect officials to **represent** their interests and serve as their voice in government. These officials must respect the wishes and opinions of the people they represent, or they will probably not be re-elected. Decision-making is often slow in a representative democracy because so many people are involved in the process. Rights and liberties are guaranteed and both the government and the people follow the law.

Monarchy

A monarchy is a government ruled by a king or queen. In an **absolute monarchy** the ruler has total power over the government and is not responsible to the people. The right to rule is **inherited**, meaning that it is passed along from a parent to a child. This serves to provide some **stability** to the government. Most monarchies today are **constitutional monarchies**.   The power of the **monarch**, or leader, is limited by a constitution, which provides for a legislature elected by the people.

Dictatorship

In some countries, one person or a small group has complete power over the government. Because of this, decision-making can be quick in times of crisis. On the other hand, the average citizen has no say in government. Elections, if they are held at all, do not offer real choices. Rights and freedoms are not guaranteed. To the contrary, most dictatorships maintain power by force and threats of violence. The government itself often ignores the law.

Activities

1. For each of the following types of governments, list an advantage and a disadvantage.

MONARCH	DICTATOR	LEGISLATURE
↓ LAWS	↓ LAWS	↕ LAWS
PEOPLE	PEOPLE	PEOPLE

Democracy

Advantage: _____

Disadvantage: _____

Monarchy

Advantage: _____

Disadvantage: _____

Dictatorship

Advantage: _____

Disadvantage: _____

FOR CLASS DISCUSSION

1. All forms of government have positive and negative features. What might be done to eliminate or reduce the negative features found in a monarchy? A dictatorship? A democracy?

2. What advantages does a constitutional monarchy have over an absolute monarchy?

3. What advantages does a representative democracy have over a direct democracy?

4. Political Parties

A **political party** is an organization of like-minded citizens who work together for common political goals. Although anyone can start a political party, the U.S. has had two major parties through most of its history. The **Federalists** and the **Anti-Federalists** were the first major parties. Today, the major parties are the **Republicans** and the **Democrats**.

Political parties do two basic things:

> 1) they **nominate**, or select, **candidates** for public office;
> 2) they develop a **platform**, or official position, on problems facing America. Each issue addressed in the platform is called a **plank**.

Every four years, the Democratic and Republican parties each hold a **national convention**. At the convention, the parties nominate candidates for President and Vice-President and develop their party's platform. The two parties also meet at state and local levels to nominate candidates to run for other public offices. Candidates from the same party compete in a **primary election**. The winner, or **nominee**, then runs against the winner from the other party in the **general election**.

Political parties make it easier for voters to elect leaders. Most voters have a sense for the general platforms of the major parties. In general, Republicans are known for their conservative approach to issues while Democrats tend to support liberal positions. Many people vote for candidates on the basis of their membership in a party.

Liberals	Conservatives
• tend to favor change	• tend to be cautious about change
• believe government should take an active role in social reform	• believe government should stay out of the affairs of private citizens and businesses as much as possible
• stress the idea of social equality	• stress private enterprise, business

Most people elected to major offices in the U.S. are members of a party. However, you do not have to belong to a party to vote in a general election or to run for office. A person who is not a party member is called an **independent**.

Third parties form in our country from time to time to address special issues. These parties are sometimes absorbed into existing parties. **Radical** political groups have never gained much power in U.S. politics. Radicals favor rapid, fundamental changes in society and are generally extreme in their views.

Activities

1. If you and a group of classmates were running for student council positions in your school, what issues might you address? Write a platform for your "political party" that contains three or more planks.

2. In political slang, the word "left" is associated with liberal views, the word "right" with conservative views. Arrange the words below from left to right on the lines provided to show how various positions relate to each other. One word should appear twice.

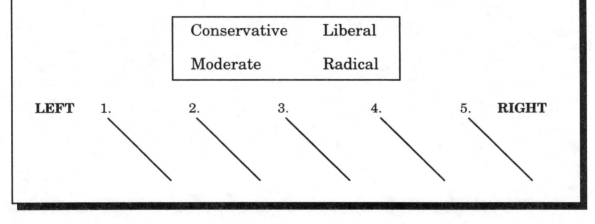

Conservative	Liberal
Moderate	Radical

LEFT   1. _____   2. _____   3. _____   4. _____   5. _____   **RIGHT**

1. Why is it difficult for independent candidates to get elected to major offices in the United States?

2. What is the difference between a primary election and a general election?

3. Do you think it is a good idea to vote for a candidate on the basis of his or her membership in a certain political party? Why or why not?

5. Role of Public Officials

How Public Officials Get Their Jobs:

Government officials get their jobs in one of two ways:

1. they are **elected** by voters; or,

2. they are **appointed** by another official or government agency.

At the national level, the only officials elected by voters are the President, the Vice-President, Senators, and Representatives. Senators and Representatives are elected directly by the people. The President and Vice-President are elected by the **electoral college**. Voters in each state choose **electors** to represent them in the college. The electors then vote for president and vice-president. The names of the presidential and vice-presidential candidates appear on the ballot in most states, including Ohio, even though voters do not directly elect the candidates.

The President appoints many important national officials, including members of the **Cabinet**, the **Supreme Court**, and ambassadors to foreign countries. Appointments must be confirmed by the Senate.

At the state level in Ohio, the Governor, the Attorney General, the Secretary of State, the State Senators and Representatives, and the state judges are all directly elected by voters. Many state officials are appointed by the governor.

At local levels, many officials are often elected, including mayors, city council members, city attorneys, municipal court judges, county commissioners, and members of county boards. (In some local governments, many of these positions are appointed.)

Evaluating Officials

All officials, whether elected or appointed, are in office to work for the common good of the people. It is up to the people, then, to make sure they have good men and women in office. Voters can read newspapers, watch TV, and listen to the radio to know what is being said about public officials or candidates for office. Attending meetings where candidates appear is a good way to learn more about their views.

People use different **criteria** in evaluating the **performance** of officials. The following questions provide an overview of the types of questions that might be asked in evaluating an official.

- Does the official have strong **leadership** qualities? Do you think he or she succeeds in getting people working together toward common goals?

- Does the official have strong **management** qualities? Does he or she seem organized and decisive enough to handle the responsibilities and problems of office?

- Has the official made good decisions since taking office?

- Does the official relate well to the public, in an open, honest manner?

FOR CLASS DISCUSSION

1. What advantages are there to electing, rather than appointing, government officials?

2. What advantage might there be to the fact that many officials are appointed?

3. Some people have suggested that the presidency should be an appointive position. What concerns would you have about this process?

4. What is the difference between the way the President and Vice-President are elected and the way Senators and Representatives are elected?

Activities:

1. How do government officials get their jobs in your area? For each of the positions listed below that apply to your community, find out if the official is elected or appointed, then mark an 'X' in the appropriate category.

Position	Elected	Appointed
Mayor / City Manager		
City or Village Council Member		
City Attorney		
Municipal Court Judge		
County Commissioner		
Chief of Police		

2. If you were asked to develop a "score card" for evaluating government officials, what qualities or skills would you list as the 5 most important? Write your answer in the spaces below, then briefly explain why you chose that particular quality or skill.

Quality or Skill	Reason for selecting it
1. _____	_____
2. _____	_____
3. _____	_____
4. _____	_____
5. _____	_____

Questions for Review

A. Vocabulary

_____ 1. elects the President and Vice-President

_____ 2. powers held by the national government

_____ 3. the position on a single issue in a party's platform

_____ 4. guarantees that no one branch of government gets too powerful

_____ 5. government by elected officials

_____ 6. not a member of a major political party

_____ 7. powers shared by the state and federal governments

_____ 8. government with a hereditary ruler

_____ 9. powers held by the state

_____ 10. system that divides powers between national and state governments

_____ 11. a party's overall position on problems facing the country

A. separation of powers

B. platform

C. representational democracy

D. reserved

E. monarchy

F. concurrent

G. federalism

H. plank

I. delegated powers

J. independent

K. electoral college

B. Completion

1. In the United States' system of government, the _____ branch makes the law, the _____ branch enforces the law, and the _____ branch interprets the law.

2. The three levels of government are _____, _____, and _____.

3. Two types of government where one person could have complete power are a _____ and a _____.

4. The first major political parties in the U.S. were the _____ and the

   _____.

5. The two major political parties in the U.S. today are the _____ and

   the _____.

6. Candidates from the same party compete for their party's nomination in a

   _____ election.

7. _____ believe the government should play a strong part in social

   reform, while _____ believe government should stay out of the

   affairs of private citizens and business as much as possible.

C. True or False

_____ 1. The three branches of government operate at all levels of government.

_____ 2. Only the national government has the power to tax citizens.

_____ 3. In an absolute monarchy, a constitution provides for a legislature elected by the people.

_____ 4. Senators and Representatives are elected by popular vote.

_____ 5. Most dictators are secure enough in their power to allow criticism of the government by the public and press.

_____ 6. Most state governors are appointed by the President.

_____ 7. No special permission is needed to start a political party.

D. Short Answer

1. The Democrats and Republicans hold national conventions every four years. What are the two main purposes of those conventions?

   _____

   _____

2. How do monarchs, such as kings or queens, receive the right to rule?

_____

3. What are the two ways government officials in the U.S. get their jobs?

_____

4. How is the concept of federalism related to levels of government?

_____

5. What is a basic disadvantage of a representative democracy?

_____

E. Multiple Choice

1. All of the following are powers delegated to the federal government EXCEPT
   A. printing money.
   B. conducting elections.
   C. establishing post offices.
   D. declaring war.

2. Which of the following is an employee of the executive branch of government?
   A. a Supreme Court justice
   B. a Senator in the Ohio legislature
   C. a member of the U.S. House of Representatives
   D. a Cincinnati police officer

3. Ellen attended a parade in honor of the queen of her country in the morning. In the afternoon, she voted for her favorite candidate for the national legislature. What type of government does Ellen's country have?
   A. a constitutional monarchy
   B. a representational democracy
   C. a dictatorship
   D. an absolute monarchy

Extended Activities

1. Branches of Government

Imagine that you have been chosen to take an extraterrestrial on a tour of government in our country. You may choose to show the extraterrestrial either one level of government or one branch of government. What is important for the extraterrestrial to know (and possibly to see) in order to understand our form of government?

2. Federalism

Hold a debate between two groups of students playing the part of people living in post-Revolutionary War America. The Articles of Confederation are in effect, but some people are talking about the need for a stronger central government and also about writing a Constitution. One group is in favor of keeping things the way they are. The other group is in favor of a Constitution and a stronger central government. The people debating should give the pros and cons of each point of view.

3. Types of Government

Imagine that you work for a magazine-format TV program like *60 Minutes*. You are to interview a head of state from either a monarchy, a dictatorship, or a democracy. Choose a real head of state if possible. Plan the interview. What kinds of things do you want to ask this person? What kinds of things do you think the person will want to talk about concerning his or her job?

4. Political Parties

Imagine that you and some friends have decided to start a new national political party. Name your party. What is your platform? How will you gather support for your party on the local, state, and national levels?

5. Role of Public Officials

A. Invite a local public official to talk to your class about what he or she does, how decisions are made on the local level, current local issues, what makes a good community leader, etc.

B. Examine the voting record of one of your Representatives or Senators. Analyze his or her voting pattern. How many times did he/she abstain, miss roll call, vote in favor of/against spending, etc.? Write a letter to this person expressing your specific approval/ disapproval of his/her voting record and explain why you think as you do.

Test Writers' Workshop

Use the diagram to develop questions 1–3.

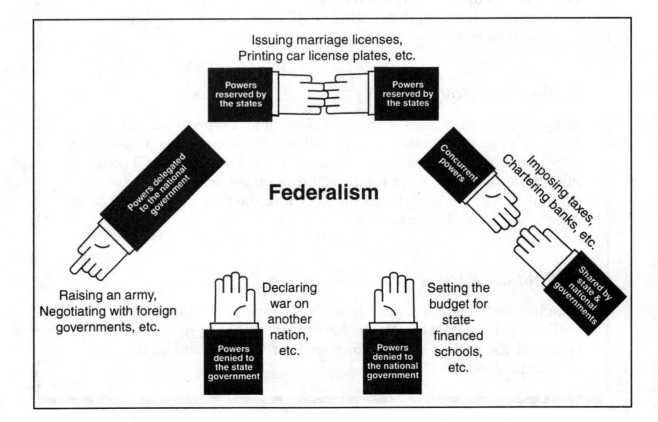

Issuing marriage licenses, Printing car license plates, etc.

Powers reserved by the states

Powers reserved by the states

Powers delegated to the national government

Concurrent powers

Imposing taxes, Chartering banks, etc.

Federalism

Shared by state & national governments

Raising an army, Negotiating with foreign governments, etc.

Declaring war on another nation, etc.

Powers denied to the state government

Setting the budget for state-financed schools, etc.

Powers denied to the national government

Complete the following multiple-choice test question about the information in the diagram by creating the missing answer choices.

1. Which of the following is an example of a power that is **reserved** by the states?

   A. _____

   B. _____

   C. _____

   D. _____

   Hint: Be sure that *only* the correct answer choice is reserved by the states. Incorrect answer choices should be selected from the other categories, such as "powers shared by the states and the national government."

Now write two more complete multiple-choice items using the information in the diagram.

2. _____

   _____

   A. _____

   B. _____

   C. _____

   D. _____

3. _____

   _____

   A. _____

   B. _____

   C. _____

   D. _____

LAW

citizenship review

Within the category of law, the Ohio State Department of Education expects you to know about the following topics:

1. Making and Amending Laws

Students will be required to describe the process for making, amending, or removing laws. Topics will include:

- the sequence of steps for making laws in the United States Congress and in the Ohio General Assembly;
- the process for amending or removing laws, either by constitutional amendment, the passage of other laws, or judicial review;
- the process for amending the U.S. Constitution;
- the process of initiative petition (requesting a new law) and referendum (the acceptance or rejection of a new law by voters) in Ohio.

2. Protection Under the Law

The student will be expected to know how the law protects individuals in the United States. The student should be able to:

- give examples of rights and freedoms guaranteed in the Bill of Rights;
- apply the concept of justice, including due process and equity before the law;
- know the importance of a learning or work environment free of discrimination against individual differences;
- identify legal means of dissent and protest against violation of rights.

1. Making and Amending Laws

Making a law

Every law begins as a **bill**. At the national level, only a **legislator** (meaning a member of the U.S. Congress) can **introduce** a bill. Congress is composed of the **Senate** and the **House of Representatives**. Only a **senator** can introduce a bill in the Senate. Only a **congressman** or **congresswoman** can introduce a bill in the House of Representatives.

Other people and groups, however, may suggest bills. The executive branch of the U.S. Government suggests many bills to Congress. Not even the President, however, has the power to introduce a bill. Many bills are written by **pressure groups** (also called **special interest groups** or **political action committees**) from such areas as education, business, industry, and agriculture.

At the state level, Ohio voters may propose a new law through an **"initiative petition."** A **petition** describing the law is presented to qualified voters. If ten percent of them sign the petition, then the bill must be put before all voters, who then decide if they want it to become law.

After a bill is **introduced** in the **legislature** (or lawmaking body), it must go through a step-by-step process to become a law. The flow chart below is a simplified version of how a bill becomes a law.

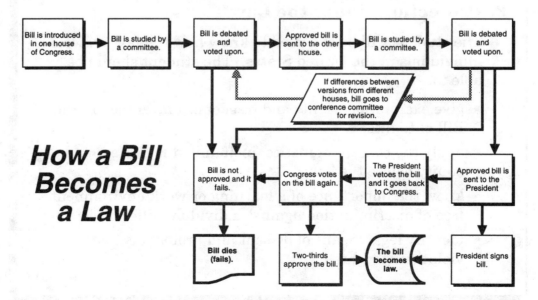

How a Bill Becomes a Law

The process for making a law in the Ohio **General Assembly** is very similar. Once the bill is approved by both houses, it is sent to the governor, who may sign the bill, veto it, or refuse to take action. If the governor refuses to sign the bill within 10 working days, it becomes law. If the governor vetoes the bill, it goes back to the state legislature. The legislature can **override** the governor's veto by a 3/5 vote in each house.

Most bills do not survive the **legislative** process. For example, in 1990 about 13,000 bills were introduced in Congress. Only 404 became law. The process was deliberately made difficult so that only strongly supported bills can become law.

Amending or removing a law

Sometimes a law is passed that later needs to be changed, or **amended**. Other times laws may need to be removed, or **abolished**. This can happen in several ways.

- The legislature may approve an amendment to an existing law, or it may pass a new law which replaces the old law.
- Laws may be ruled **unconstitutional** through a process called **judicial review**. If the Supreme Court declares a law unconstitutional, it means the law itself is illegal.
- Citizens may request a change in the law through **petition** (previously described). Laws already passed by the legislature must be presented to the voters for approval. This process is called a **referendum**.
- Amendments to the U.S. Constitution can be **proposed** in two ways:
    1) Congress can propose an amendment by a two-thirds vote of each house.
    2) If two-thirds of the state legislatures vote to request an amendment, Congress must call a national convention to formally propose it. This method has never been used.
- Proposed amendments must be **ratified** (approved) to become law. They may be ratified in two ways:
    1) The legislatures in three-fourths of the states can ratify the amendment.
    2) Conventions in three-fourths of the states can ratify the amendment.

In the past 200 years, the Constitution has only been amended 26 times. The 21st Amendment, which repealed Prohibition, was the only amendment ratified by state conventions.

Activities:

1. Complete the following chart to make sure you understand some basic differences between lawmaking at the federal and the state level.

	Ohio	Federal
Name of legislative body:		
Official who signs or vetoes:		
Fraction of legislative vote needed to override veto:		

2. Imagine that you are a senator in your state legislature. You are interested in getting a law passed that would give students an annual "Spring Fever" holiday on the first Friday of spring. What steps would you have to follow? Number the steps below in proper sequence, from 1 to 11.

___ governor signs or vetoes bill

___ bill introduced in Senate

___ bill is debated and approved by House

___ bill is studied by a Senate committee

___ bill is sent to governor

___ bill is sent to House

___ bill is studied by House committee

___ legislature overrides veto with 3/5 vote or bill dies

___ bill is sent to conference committee

___ bill is debated and approved by Senate

___ if vetoed, bill is sent back to legislature

FOR CLASS DISCUSSION

1. Why doesn't the President have the power to introduce a bill?

2. What are the disadvantages of pressure groups? What are the advantages?

3. What are some ways that average citizens can be involved in the lawmaking process?

2. Protection Under the Law

The Bill of Rights

When the Constitution was written, many states refused to approve it unless individual rights were guaranteed. The Bill of Rights, which consists of the first ten amendments to the Constitution, was added in 1791. Below is an abbreviated list of the rights and freedoms guaranteed by those amendments:

Amendment One guarantees freedom of speech, religion, **press**, **assembly**, and **petition**.

Amendment Two guarantees the right of states to organize militias, or armies, and the right of individuals to bear arms.

Amendment Three prohibits the **quartering** (or housing) of soldiers in private homes during peacetime.

Amendment Four prohibits unreasonable search and **seizure** (taking complete control of a person's property).

Amendment Five prohibits an accused person from having to testify against him- or herself (**self-incrimination**); bans **double jeopardy**, which means being tried for the same crime twice; and guarantees that no person will suffer the loss of life, liberty, or property without **due process** of law.

Amendment Six guarantees the right to a speedy, public trial by an impartial jury; the right to a lawyer; the right to cross-examine witnesses; and the right to force witnesses to appear at a trial to testify (known as a **subpoena**).

Amendment Seven guarantees the right to a jury trial in civil suits. (Civil suits are court proceedings between two individuals or businesses.)

Amendment Eight prohibits cruel and unusual punishment and excessive bail and fines.

Amendment Nine identifies powers reserved for the people.

Amendment Ten identifies powers reserved for the states.

Due Process of Law

The Fifth Amendment of the Bill of Rights states that no person "shall be deprived of life, liberty, or property without due process of law." This means that the government must follow the same rules whenever anyone is accused of a crime or is involved in a civil suit. Rights of the individual include: the right to a trial by jury, the right to a lawyer, and the right to a speedy trial.

Later amendments were added to the Constitution to expand on the definition of due process and to win equal treatment for all Americans:

The 14th Amendment (1868)

- Defines citizenship.
- Guarantees all citizens "equal protection under the law."
- Guarantees due process of law.

The 15th Amendment (1870)

- Grants the right to become a U.S. citizen to all individuals, regardless of race or color.
- Extends the right to vote to African American males.

The 19th Amendment (1920)

- Gives women the right to vote.

The 26th Amendment (1971)

- Changed the voting age from 21 to 18.

Discrimination

Discrimination occurs when a person or group is treated differently from other persons and groups, usually on the basis of race, religion, nationality, or sex. Discrimination also occurs against people with handicaps, such as hearing, speech, or vision disorders, or diseases, such as muscular dystrophy.

Discrimination is usually a result of **prejudice**. Prejudice occurs when someone forms a judgment or opinion without knowing the facts. For example, an unfair, negative attitude toward an entire group of people may be formed on the basis of some group characteristic. Prejudice based on race is called **racism**. Prejudice based on **gender** is called **sexism.**

The 14th Amendment guarantees all U.S. citizens "equal protection of the law." Therefore, discrimination based on religion, race, or sex is unconstitutional, or illegal. Lawsuits can be filed against the government or businesses for unfair discrimination.

The U.S. Government has addressed the problem of racism in our country by making **segregation** (a separation of blacks and whites) illegal in public schools and facilities. In addition to this effort at **integration**, the government has also enacted **affirmative action** programs for government and business. These programs require that organizations take steps to increase the number or proportion of its members who are **minorities**.

Legal Dissent

In many countries, people are imprisoned, tortured, and even executed for criticizing their leaders and government. In the United States, the right to **dissent**, or disagree, is guaranteed by the First Amendment.

The law provides ways for people to legally dissent. Citizens may **petition** government leaders, file **lawsuits**, or join marches, sit-ins, or boycotts as a means of legal protest.

Not all forms of dissent are legal. Sometimes people will break a law on purpose in an effort to get that law changed. For example, some people in the past have trespassed on government military bases to protest nuclear arms. This type of illegal, but usually peaceful, dissent is called **civil disobedience**.

Activities:

1. The Bill of Rights is as important to our society today as it was in 1791 when it was written. For each of the situations listed below, identify the Amendment that guarantees that particular right or freedom.

   A. A newspaper publishes an editorial attacking the President's stand on an environmental issue. Amendment # _____.

   B. A suspect who has been arrested and accused of a crime is released on bail. Amendment # _____.

   C. A group of citizens organize a peaceful march on the nation's Capitol to draw attention to the problem of homelessness in America. Amendment #_____.

   D. The defendant in a criminal trial refuses to testify against himself. Amendment # _____.

   E. A person facing criminal charges cannot afford a lawyer, so the court assigns him one. Amendment # _____.

2. The right for all registered, adult citizens of the U.S. to vote is based on several Amendments to the Constitution. Connect the Amendments on the left with the appropriate group of people on the right.

The 15th Amendment	18-year-olds
The 19th Amendment	women
The 26th Amendment	African American men

3. Legal dissent and civil disobedience are two ways of protesting. If your school started a new policy you did not agree with, such as a new dress code, what would be an example of "legal" dissent? What would be an example of "civil disobedience"?

FOR CLASS DISCUSSION

1. In our country, criticizing the government is not only allowed, it is considered a basic right of the individual. What effect, if any, do you think open criticism has on the quality of a government?

2. Why would a person or group use civil disobedience as a means of protest instead of a legal form of dissent?

Questions for Review

A. Vocabulary

_____ 1. a lawmaking body

_____ 2. to protest a law by breaking it

_____ 3. a member of the House of Representatives

_____ 4. to change or add to an existing law

_____ 5. to present a law to voters for approval

_____ 6. the lawmaking body of Ohio

_____ 7. the lawmaking body of the U.S.

_____ 8. when a law itself is declared illegal

_____ 9. treating a person differently on the basis of a group characteristic

_____ 10. to disagree

_____ 11. prejudice based on gender

A. dissent

B. General Assembly

C. referendum

D. amend

E. sexism

F. discrimination

G. Congressman

H. legislature

I. Congress

J. unconstitutional

K. civil disobedience

70

B. Completion

1. Only a member of _____ can introduce a bill at the national level.

2. If the Governor of Ohio vetoes a bill, the General Assembly can _____ the decision by a _____ vote in each house.

3. A new amendment to the Constitution must be ratified by _____ of the states.

4. In the United States, our right to criticize the government is guaranteed by the _____ Amendment.

5. The first ten amendments to the Constitution are known as _____.

6. The Supreme Court may rule a law unconstitutional through a process called _____.

7. The Fifth Amendment to the Constitution states that no person "shall be deprived of _____, _____, or _____ without due process of law."

C. True or False

_____ 1. Many laws are introduced in Congress by the President.

_____ 2. Ohio voters can propose a new law by using a petition process.

_____ 3. Double jeopardy means two people cannot be tried for the same crime.

_____ 4. The Bill of Rights extended the right to vote to women.

_____ 5. It is possible for a legislature to pass a law that is illegal.

_____ 6. Most bills introduced in Congress are signed into law.

_____ 7. The courts can force a witness to a crime to appear and testify at a trial.

D. Short Answer

1. What happens to a bill if the President vetoes it?

   _____

2. Briefly describe the purpose and process of an "initiative petition" in Ohio.

   _____

   _____

3. What is the goal of "affirmative action"?

   _____

4. Name three forms of dissent or protest that are legal in the United States.

   1) _____ 2) _____ 3) _____

5. Name three ways that a law can be amended or removed:

   1) _____

   2) _____

   3) _____

E. Multiple Choice

1. Which of the following steps could not actually occur in the lawmaking process at the national level?
   A. A special interest group writes a bill which is then introduced by a Congressman.
   B. A bill is debated and approved by the Senate before being sent to the House of Representatives.
   C. A bill is debated and rejected in the House without ever going to the Senate.
   D. The President signs a bill into law, but Congress chooses to override his decision.

2. In 1872, a U.S. citizen votes in a presidential election for the first time. This person could NOT have been
   A. born in another country.
   B. a woman.
   C. a freed slave.
   D. a 21-year-old.

3. A man is accused of stealing a bike. Which of the following would be a violation of his Constitutional rights?
   A. He is arrested without a lawyer present.
   B. He is put in jail and not released until his bail is set and paid.
   C. He is assigned a lawyer he has never met or heard of before.
   D. At his trial the judge orders him to say whether or not he stole the bike.

Extended Activities

1. Making and Amending Laws

A. Imagine that you and your classmates are either state legislators or U.S. Congressmen and Congresswomen. Introduce a bill, send it through committee, debate it on the floor in the general session, and finally vote on it. Some students should represent people in favor of the bill and others should play the role of opponents of the bill.

B. Take a position on a current or proposed amendment to the Constitution and defend it. Use newspaper and magazine articles to support your position. Make a videotape (or audio tape) of your commentary for a TV or radio editorial. If you feel strongly about the issue, check with your local cable TV station to see if their community access channel might play your tape.

2. Protection Under the Law

A. Bring a news article to class that is related in some way to one of the Bill of Rights amendments. Discuss the article in class. Is this right being upheld, threatened, or abused?

B. Research one or more of the following people and their views on civil disobedience: Ralph Waldo Emerson, Henry David Thoreau, Jean Jacques Rousseau, Leo Tolstoy, Martin Luther King, and Mohandas Gandhi. Hold a class discussion comparing the views of these people.

Test Writers' Workshop

Use the explanation of the Bill of Rights on page 66 to develop questions 1–3.

Read the following paragraph. Then complete the multiple-choice test question about the Bill of Rights by creating the missing answer choices.

> Police officer Celia Noble caught Simon White inside of the Acme Warehouse after hours. She found a broken window near the back door and tiny pieces of glass on Simon's gloves. As far as Celia could tell, Simon had not stolen anything. She arrested him for breaking and entering. The next morning, Simon's lawyer got him released from jail because he said Celia had not "read Simon his rights" when she arrested him.

1. Which amendment was Officer Noble accused of violating?

   A. _____

   B. _____

   C. _____

   D. _____

Hint: First write in the correct amendment. Then write the incorrect choices so that all the amendments in the answer choices are listed in numerical order.

Now write two more complete multiple-choice items based on the information given below.

Rudyard Barnes was accused of embezzling a million dollars from the Trustworthy Savings and Loan Association. Before the trial, the district attorney sent a message to Rudyard's boss, Ellen Simple, at Trustworthy. The message told Ms. Simple to appear in court to testify against Rudyard. When Ms. Simple refused, the District Attorney had her arrested. After a lengthy trial, the jury found that there was not enough evidence to convict Rudyard, even though they believed him to be guilty of the crime. When the jury foreman read the verdict of "Not guilty," Rudyard smiled. Later, he was heard outside the courtroom telling his lawyer that he took the money, but there was nothing anyone could do about it now.

2. _____

_____

A. _____

B. _____

C. _____

D. _____

3. _____

_____

A. _____

B. _____

C. _____

D. _____

CITIZEN KNOWLEDGE

citizenship review

Within the category of citizen knowledge, the Ohio State Department of Education expects you to know the following topics:

1. Voting responsibility and privilege

Students will be expected to know that voting is both a privilege and a responsibility of U.S. citizenship. Topics will include:

- the qualifications for voting
- recognizing that property ownership, race, gender, literacy, and certain tax payments no longer affect eligibility to vote

2. Using sources of information

Students should be able to use information that enables citizens to make informed choices. Required skills include:

- using more than one source to obtain information
- identifying points of agreement and disagreement among sources
- evaluating the reliability of available information
- drawing conclusions by reading and interpreting data presented in graphs and charts
- identifying and weighing alternative viewpoints

3. Opportunities for civic involvement

Students will be expected to understand the concept of citizenship as a participatory activity.

1. Voting Responsibility and Privilege

In a democracy, the power of government ultimately belongs to the people. The way people in the United States exercise their power is through voting. The power to vote is called **suffrage**, or "the franchise." The United States is a representative democracy where voters elect many of the government officials who are responsible for making, enforcing, and interpreting laws. These government officials obtain their power through the voters.

In Ohio, voters may propose a new law through an **initiative**. An initiative is an electoral procedure that allows citizens to propose a law and place it on the ballot by obtaining signatures from registered voters on a petition. Ohio residents may also vote on whether or not to pass new laws through a **referendum**. A referendum presents laws passed by the state legislature to voters for approval.

Because of the power that goes with voting, it is both a responsibility and a privilege. People who could vote but don't, give up that power to those who do.

Before 1870, only white males who were 21 years of age or older could vote in most areas of the U.S. Many areas also required that voters own property. These and other restrictions have been dropped over the years, as summarized below:

- The 15th Amendment (1870) extended the right to vote to African American men.

- The 19th Amendment (1920) extended the right to vote to women.

- The 24th Amendment (1964) stated that a person cannot be required to own property or pay a **poll tax** in order to vote.

- The Voting Rights Act (1965) abolished **literacy tests** as a requirement for voting.

- The 26th Amendment (1971) lowered the legal voting age to 18.

Today, to qualify to vote in Ohio, you must be:

- a U.S. citizen

- a resident of Ohio

- at least 18 years of age* by the November election

- registered with the board of elections

- a resident of your voting precinct for 30 days prior to the election

* In Ohio, 17-year-olds who will be 18 by the November election may vote for candidates in primary elections. They may also vote on all issues except those involving money.

Activities:

1. The chart below shows reasons why people in the U.S. say they don't vote. Study the chart, then discuss which reasons you think are good ones and which ones sound more like excuses to you. You might also discuss other possible reasons why people don't vote. After you've done that, develop a list of reasons why people *should* vote.

WHY PEOPLE DON'T VOTE   WHY PEOPLE SHOULD VOTE

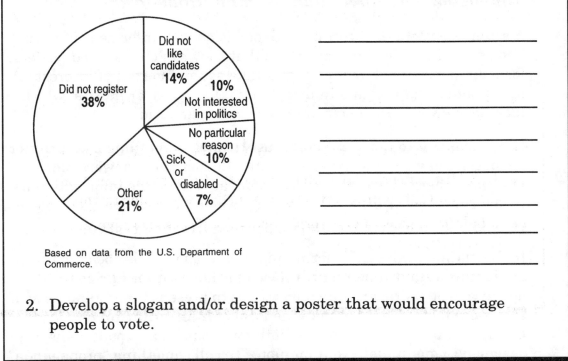

Based on data from the U.S. Department of Commerce.

2. Develop a slogan and/or design a poster that would encourage people to vote.

FOR CLASS DISCUSSION

1. In the U.S., one-third of all eligible voters are not registered. Less than one-half of those who are registered vote in most elections. In some countries, such as Italy and Australia, it's against the law not to vote. Do you think the U.S. should have a law making it a crime not to vote? Why or why not?

2. What is the difference between an initiative and a referendum? Why are these processes important to average citizens?

2. Using Sources of Information

The media and other sources of information

A strong democratic government depends on well-informed citizens. People need reliable information so that they can choose good leaders, form opinions on public issues, and take action in areas of interest. A major source of news and information is the **press**, or **media**, which includes newspapers, magazines, television, and radio.

It is important to remember that just because something is in print or on TV doesn't always mean it is accurate. Readers and viewers must **evaluate** the source of the information, as well as the information itself, to determine **reliability**. Comparing two or more sources is a good way to get a balanced view of a subject, especially if it is controversial.

In evaluating sources of information, readers must also be able to distinguish a **fact** from an **opinion**. Obviously, it is often to the advantage of politicians and advertisers to present their opinions as if they were facts. This can take the form of **manipulation** or **propaganda**. Advertisements, both for products and politicians, are designed to manipulate your opinion. To call something "propaganda" does not necessarily mean that it is false, but that it is a one-sided view. Groups **disseminate** propaganda to help their own cause. Sometimes this also includes hurting their opponents, often through misleading or incomplete information.

In order to get a fair picture of a particular topic or event, it is usually a good idea to check several news or information sources. The **electronic media** (radio and TV) are good at delivering news of fast-breaking events and at summarizing current events of the day. The **print media** (newspapers and magazines) are good at providing more in-depth coverage of issues that might be of interest to you. Some of the better sources of information are listed below:

Common sources of information:

- the daily newspaper in your community

- local and national TV news programs

- weekly news magazines, such as *Time* and *Newsweek*

- television "magazine style" news programs, such as *60 Minutes* or *20/20*

- *The New York Times*, a daily newspaper with a national reputation

- television and radio news programs, such as *Meet the Press*

- public radio and public television news and "magazine" programs

- reference books, such as almanacs, encyclopedias, and atlases

Activities:

1. Using an article from a current newspaper or news magazine, identify three examples of fact and three of opinion.

   Source: _____

   Facts:

   A. _____

   B. _____

   C. _____

   Opinions:

   A. _____

   B. _____

   C. _____

2. Identify two articles in current newspapers or news magazines that present opposing viewpoints on a single issue. (The editorial pages of daily newspapers are a good place to locate such articles.)

3. For each of the following sources of information, name an advantage and a disadvantage:

	Advantage	Disadvantage
a daily newspaper		
a national TV news program		
a monthly magazine		
a radio interview program		
an almanac		

FOR CLASS DISCUSSION

1. If you were trying to get information on a political candidate, what would be the pros and cons of the following sources of information?

    • the candidate's own TV commercials

    • a newspaper article presenting the candidate's views on specific issues

    • letters and brochures mailed to you by the candidate's campaign committee

    • a television debate between the candidate and his or her opponent

    • a newspaper editorial endorsing the candidate

2. Advertising—including political advertising—can be very informative and interesting. But is it a good idea to base a decision, such as to buy a product or vote for a candidate, on advertising alone? Why or why not?

Reading charts and graphs

Information, especially quantitative **data**, is often presented visually. There are several basic types of charts and graphs, as illustrated below. Most charts and graphs are fairly easy to read, if you know what you're looking for.

Circle Graph

A **circle graph**, also known as a **pie graph**, shows how something (such as money or time) is divided. Each "slice" of the pie is a percentage of the whole. Large percentages show up as big slices. Small percentages become small slices. Percentages within the pie can be compared by comparing the size of the slices.

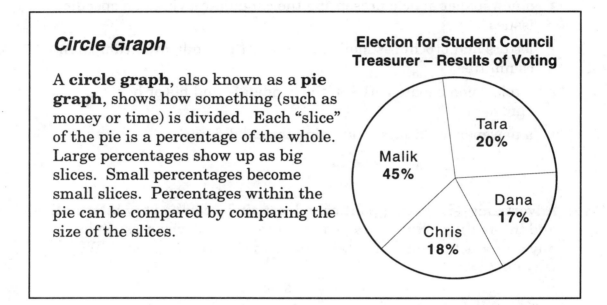

Election for Student Council Treasurer – Results of Voting

Tara 20%
Malik 45%
Dana 17%
Chris 18%

To read a circle graph, you should:

- find out what the overall graph represents by checking the **title** (such as Election for Student Council Treasurer—Results of Voting);

- find out what each slice means by checking its **label** (such as each student's name: Tara, Malik, Dana, Chris);

- know what you are looking for within the graph by examining the question.

Bar Graph

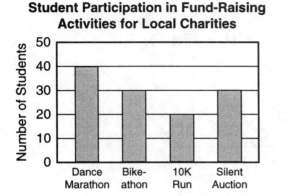

A bar graph compares the value of related things.

Line Graph

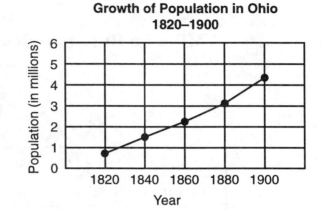

A line graph shows changes or trends over time.

To read a bar or line graph, you should:

- find out what the whole graph is about by checking the title;

- make sure you understand what is being marked on the **horizontal axis** (the left to right, or flat, axis);

- make sure you understand what is being marked on the **vertical axis** (the one that goes up and down);

- make sure you know what type of measuring units (such as days, feet, number of people) are being used;

- know what you are looking for within the graph by examining the question.

On most bar graphs, one axis will show measuring units and the other will show a **variable** that is being measured.

Charts or Tables

Mileage Between Several Cities in Ohio

	Akron	Cincinnati	Cleveland	Columbus	Toledo	Youngstown
Akron	—	235	37	126	124	50
Cincinnati	235	—	249	111	210	278
Cleveland	37	249	—	144	116	77
Columbus	126	111	144	—	144	170
Toledo	124	210	116	144	—	170
Youngstown	50	278	77	170	170	—

Charts and tables are often used to present numbers in a way that is easy to read and understand. Each box of information on a chart is called a **cell**. A cell can be identified by the number or name of its column and row. (For example, "row 3, column 4" from the chart identifies the cell with the number 144, which is the number of miles from Cleveland to Columbus.)

To read a chart or table, you should:

- make sure you understand what the whole graph is about by reading the title;

- find out what variable is being marked in the rows;

- find out what variable is being marked in the columns;

- know what you are looking for within the graph by examining the question.

Activities:

1. Use the graphs on the previous three pages to answer the questions below.

In the **circle graph**:

Which student received the most votes? _____

Which student earned 20 percent of the votes? _____

About how many votes did Dana and Tara receive together? (Circle your answer):

      one-half   one-third   three-fourths

In the **bar graph**:

Which fund-raising activity attracts the most students? _____

About how many students participated in the Bike-athon? _____

Which two activities attracted the same number of students?

_____

In the **line graph:**

How many years have been charted so far on the graph? _____

About how many people lived in Ohio in 1880? _____

Which period of time showed the greatest population increase in Ohio?

_____

In the **table:**

Which two cities are farthest from each other? _____

What is the distance between Columbus and Cleveland? _____

What would be the round-trip distance between Youngstown and

Akron? _____

3. Opportunities for Civic Involvement

Knowing about issues is just the start of being a good citizen. In the United States, citizenship also means getting involved. Our society offers citizens many opportunities to share their ideas and make changes for the better in their community, state, nation, or even the world.

Ways to get involved:

- vote
- work for a political candidate or cause
- work for or against legislation
- join political or service organizations
- write to government officials
- write a letter to the editor of your local newspaper
- run for political office yourself

Our democratic form of government depends on people who are willing to actively participate in the process. The privilege of being a citizen in a free country carries with it the responsibility of being an involved citizen.

Activities:

1. We often hear people complain about a situation without considering what can be done to change or improve that situation. For each of the following, suggest something that an individual or group might do to make a difference.

   A. A community "clean-up day" has been proposed by a local citizens' group.

   _____

   B. A city council candidate you admire needs support.

   _____

   C. The city is considering closing your local public swimming pool for an extra month each year to save money.

   _____

   D. Your village or city needs to reduce the amount of garbage and waste it must dispose of.

   _____

   E. The League of Women Voters is sponsoring a "meet the candidates night" in your area.

   _____

   F. The Ohio General Assembly is considering raising taxes.

   _____

   G. An environmental group is seeking support for a bill before Congress.

   _____

   H. A new toxic waste dump could be located in your community.

   _____

2. Name three ways you can improve your local community.

   A. _____

   B. _____

   C. _____

FOR CLASS DISCUSSION

1. What personal benefits might someone gain by becoming involved in his or her community?

2. A popular slogan in the environmental movement is "Think global, act local." What does this mean?

3. What is the relationship between civic involvement and staying informed?

Questions for Review

A. Vocabulary

_____ 1. the power to vote

_____ 2. in Ohio, presenting a new law to voters for approval

_____ 3. radio and television

_____ 4. to distribute or spread

_____ 5. a communication that presents a one-sided view and is meant to manipulate

_____ 6. a box of information on a chart

_____ 7. signed up to vote

_____ 8. information presented in the form of a sliced pie

_____ 9. newspapers and magazines

_____ 10. something that is not fixed in value, but changes

_____ 11. the vertical or horizontal line on a bar or line graph

A. disseminate

B. print media

C. propaganda

D. registered

E. circle graph

F. variable

G. suffrage

H. axis

I. referendum

J. cell

K. electronic media

90

B. Completion

1. The 26th Amendment changed the minimum age for voting from _____ to _____.

2. The 19th Amendment, passed in 1920, extended the right to vote to

   _____.

3. The Voting Rights Act of 1965 abolished _____ as a requirement for voting.

4. To vote in Ohio, you must reside in your voting precinct for _____ days prior to the election.

5. A chart or table is usually organized into _____ and rows.

C. Short Answer

1. Before 1870, what were the requirements for voting in most of the U.S.?

   _____

2. Name three groups that have been given the right to vote by amendments to the Constitution.

   _____

3. What are the qualifications for voting in Ohio?

   _____

   _____

D. True or False

_____ 1. People must pass a literacy test before they can vote.

_____ 2. Voters in Ohio can reject laws passed by the state legislature.

_____ 3. In Ohio, if a 17-year-old will be 18 by the November election, he or she may register and vote in the primary.

_____ 4. Most states require that citizens pay a poll tax before voting.

_____ 5. The main purpose of propaganda is to help people make their own decisions, based on the facts.

E. Multiple Choice

1. Jane is an 18-year-old resident of Ohio. She can't vote in today's election because she

   A. can't pass the literacy test.

   C. is not a property owner.

   B. doesn't meet the age requirement.

   D. is not registered.

2. Which of the following is probably the LEAST reliable source of information concerning an election for state senator in your district?

   A. your local newspaper

   B. campaign commercials on TV

   C. a debate on radio

   D. your local TV news program

3. If plans were being made to open a new toxic waste dump in your area, which of the following would NOT be an active way to oppose it?

   A. writing a letter to your local newspaper

   B. joining a community protest group

   C. watching a TV news report on the controversy

   D. voicing your concerns at a city council meeting

F. Reading a Graph

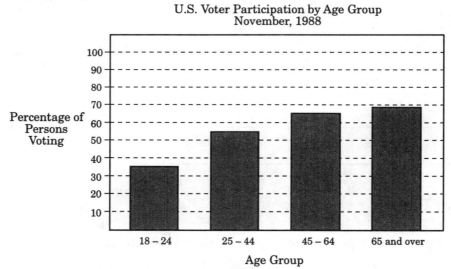

U.S. Voter Participation by Age Group
November, 1988

1. The information above is presented in the form of a

   A. pie graph

   B. table

   C. bar graph

   D. line graph

2. About what percentage of people in the 18–24 age group voted?
   A. 22%
   B. 36%
   C. 54%
   D. 62%

3. Which of the following statements about the information in the graph is true?
   A. The older the age group, the higher their participation.
   B. The younger the age group, the higher their participation.
   C. Participation was nearly equal between the youngest and oldest groups.
   D. The youngest voters and oldest voters had the best turnouts.

4. Which of the following is NOT included in the graph?
   A. the number of persons voting
   B. the ages of persons voting
   C. the percentage of persons voting
   D. the year the voting took place

5. Which age group had just slightly over half its members vote?
   A. 18–24
   B. 25–44
   C. 45–64
   D. 65 and over

Extended Activities

1. Voting Responsibility and Privilege

A. Imagine that the year is 1868. In most places in the United States only white males aged 21 or older can vote. You are (choose one): a white woman, an African American, a Mexican American, or an American Indian. Write to your Congressman telling why you should be given the right to vote.

B. Imagine that a friend of yours tells you he or she didn't bother to vote in the last general election. Write a letter to your friend and give him or her compelling reasons to register and vote in the next election.

2. Using Sources of Information

A. Find a current news article and write a "slanted" version of the same article. You may want to mix up fact and opinion. You may also leave out important information and/or add extra information. Try to fool your reading audience into thinking you are giving the straight story by making the report's biases and untruths subtle and convincing. Afterwards, trade papers with someone else in the class. Try to uncover all the ways their article was slanted.

B. Find a bar graph or line graph in a newspaper or magazine and bring it to class. Remake the graph to distort the information in it. Or, if you can find one, bring a graph to class whose information is distorted by the way the data is presented. Remake the graph to present the data in an undistorted way.

C. Examine one or more real campaign flyers or advertisements. Look for examples of propaganda. Identify actual promises versus implied promises. Identify examples of negative and positive campaign techniques. What generalizations can you make about the believability of campaign advertisements?

3. Opportunities for Civic Involvement

Find a magazine or newspaper article that describes an example of civic involvement. Participate in a class discussion about local opportunities for civic involvement. Consider questions such as: What can civic involvement require besides one's time? What are some of the obstacles to civic involvement?

Test Writers' Workshop

Use the graph for questions 1–3.

Sources of Immigrants to the United States

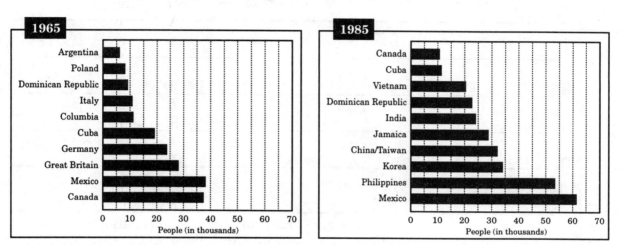

Complete the following multiple-choice test question about the information in the graph by creating the missing answer choices.

1. In 1985, most of the immigrants to the United States came from which continent?

   A. _____

   B. _____

   C. _____

   D. _____

Hint: Find the correct answer by grouping the countries represented by continent. Then, for the incorrect answer choices, write the names of three other continents represented in the two graphs.

Now write two more complete multiple-choice items using the information in the map.

2. _____

   _____

   A. _____

   B. _____

   C. _____

   D. _____

3. _____

   _____

   A. _____

   B. _____

   C. _____

   D. _____